Ceremonies of the Spirit

Wendy Brown-Báez

Plain View Press
P. O. 42255
Austin, TX 78704

plainviewpress.net
sb@plainviewpress.net
512-441-2452

Cover art *Phoenix* by Helena Nelson-Reed
Prints available at www.helenanelsonreed.com

Acknowledgements

I am grateful to the editors of the following magazines, journals and anthologies, where these poems first appeared: "Calypso" in *The Litchfield Review*; "The Sound of My Name" in *Dancing Between Worlds*; "Absence, Secrets Worth Keeping" in *Flask and Pen*; and "At el Museo, Jerusalem" in *Longing for Home* CD.

dedicated to Alejandro Báez,
for keeping the flame alive

and to all of those who believe
in miracles

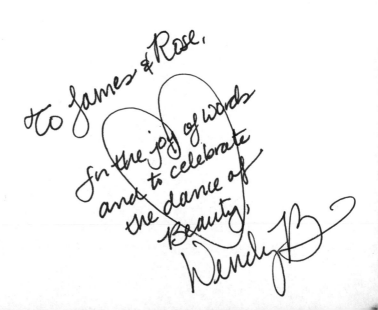

Contents

Thorn on the Rose

Surrender

Things We Lost In the Fire

Love Poems for Valentines Day and Beyond

Surrender

Consecration

Transformation

Thorn on the Rose

Certainty

It is in this moment
when I am alone
that I am most sure
that you love me.

Face to face I am consumed
with the breathless astonishment
of my body breaking away from me
running and melting
like rainbows in a puddle
whose only urge is to reach the sea.

I forget myself:
who I am and why I exist:
except for this moment
awaiting your kiss.

I am so enchanted
by the sight of your bare shoulders,
the ears above your neck,
and the dark pools of your eyes,
I don't know whether my mouth
has opened itself to speak.

It is only later,
when I am alone,
that I remember
how you leaned closer to
hear my words
how you took me
in an embrace
as brief as a shrug

leaving the mark
of my heated body
scorched all over yours.

Answering Machine

Leave your message on my machine, baby,
And your dance steps on my rug.
Steam up my bathroom mirror
And frost my thick-glassed mug.
Let your sighs fill the champagne glass
When the bubbles have escaped.
Drink my scent like soda pop
While you swing me like a gate.

When you do the locomotion, sugar,
On my body's silver rails,
I love the hear the engine spark
And the power of your wail.
The ocean liner leaving shore
Has streamers out to sea.
May the stars in your eyes, baby,
Shed their light on me.

Leave your message on my machine, baby,
And your shoes next to the door.
We'll slide down close together
Like melted marsh-mellows in a s'more.
What's the use of valentines
If you can't lick the stamp?
I'd love you all to pieces
If you just give me a chance.

Tangled Up in You

....the necessary fire,
the necessary birds that fly from
your hands as you weave
your words into my air.

Sitting too close not to touch
but determined that we won't,
unable to pass that last
semi-colon, unable to
break free of the

cocooned denial because
the flame might ignite
not only the two of us
and the very room we sit in
but the entire block

of neighbors going about their
day, the woman stirring her
vegetables, the laundry spinning
while the young man folds the
first load into neat blue piles

the child running up the steps
behind his dog, all burnt
to a shocked crisp.
Now we are tangled in
hidden meanings

and secret signals. Words make
sense for a split second
only to dance away at the least
crinkle on your face as you grin
at my unexpected boldness

Continued

and the blush I am trying so
hard to conceal has landed
in front of us on the shining
surface of the coffee table
and we pretend not to see it.

We are attempting to tango
and I am hoping not to
embarrass you by tripping in
my sexy stacked heels, the ones
I wanted you to notice

the ones I tucked away
suddenly behind my plain
black skirt.

Calypso

...and when did it begin
this sweet necessity
to know you are listening to my

salt-spray heart, rhyming tide
of ocean foam, the moon
calypsoing over my raft as it

sails away to an island of palm
trees and white doves. I sent a
continuous signal of SOS

code of revelation and urgency
not knowing if your dial was
set at my frequency. Like a dolphin

rounding the curve of its young and
nosing to the surface, did I float
free of disappointment and vanity.

Did I think when you turned
away, the soul threaded between us
snapped clear? Could I count on a

dream to pull me back, did the
open sea take me, did a fierce wind
abscond with me, scowling like a

beautiful god determined to have his own way.

Absence

I am more here in your bed
than anywhere without you.
It is after all your breath I am
breathing in the thick midnight
walls. Remembering how you told

me you wake up at three, I
awake. I need no mention
of dreams. I carry them
stillborn over the threshold
of this place so mine because

it belongs to you. Even your
past cannot creep between
us when I cradle you in my
hunger. When I stoke your
black hair like silk in my

hands, never doubting the
beat I hear is the high tide coming
to beach me on the precipice
over which I float away,
using my wings like love.

Secrets Worth Keeping

Don't listen to what they say, don't listen
to their warnings, the whispers behind their hands.

They don't know of such things as coriander seeds
being ground in the center of your being. They don't know

the little hush that falls between syllables as he gazes
into your eyes. What do they know of kisses

exchanged again and again. Don't listen to the worm of doubt
creeping into the apple of your delight, the leering

disappointment that pinches you hard under the soft
skin of your arms just when you are about

to hold them out, innocent, wanting to be filled.
Don't listen to the hag of fear cackle about the past.

She remembers the thorn in your finger when all you recall
is the blood scent of roses. Don't pay attention to

ghosts who rise up to scratch your eyes with tears
in the middle of your extravagant folly, jealous that

you forgot your sorrow for one brief moment.
Let the wind blow the dust from your palms,

let the river drift you along, lift your head as high as
your soul. Let your heart answer in riddle and rhyme.

Waking Up

to remember that you were here
to remember awakening before the light hit the room
    and breathing in the quiet
to remember I awoke in joy
    of your body asleep beside me
to remember the dreamy smiles, the sleepy kisses,
    the pulling of our bodies into each other
to remember the feel of your hands on my
    thighs under my nightgown
to remember pulling it over my head
    and how you had to help
my hair spilling out onto the pillow
    the roughness of your cheeks
the light entering our bodies
to remember the hammering of my heart under yours
to remember how you cried my name
to remember the tenderness after when we lay quiet
    when I said I love you
    when you said the same
to remember it was a day of plenty to do with as we wished
to remember how I called you my angel
to remember how you rolled a cigarette in your silk underwear
    and I floated around the kitchen in my nightgown making coffee
to remember you offered to make crepes
    and I kissed you by the dishes
to remember we were content with the discovery of how well
    we fit together with the music on the CD player
    how you loved mariachi and howled and I laughed
    how you danced with the spatula in your hand

to remember all this before the darkness came
  when all you longed for was the silence of the grave
when the gun sat waiting under the bed and I never knew it was there
  the final option, the liberation you craved
to remember there were mornings before the tears
to remember that I took back for myself my own sanctity
to remember this place beside me is empty
  and I have no way to know if it can be filled
to remember who I am and why
to remember we had a cycle and a season
  and there begins with each morning
yet another day and different reasons

The Perfect Moment

Maybe it was when you stretched out on the
couch and said, Sing me a lullaby,
the way you clutched the pillow to your chest
like a young child and I became the
mama who knew what to do for her boy.

Maybe it was when I settled myself to take your
head into my lap, the way you became the man
I had caressed those years of floating
out the evening until we could go to bed
and I would be comforted by human warmth
to mask our haunting fear.

Maybe it was the way you sank into sleep
and I watched your breath rising and falling
until my hand grew still and I fell back against the
pillow and slept as well, satisfied.

Maybe it was how you turned and I cradled you,
how the heat of our bodies lingered in my hands
and along my arm right up into my heart and
caused me to remember desire and hope.

Maybe that is why I am making it
through memory and grief, the turning
of salt water into wine.

Surrender

At El Museo

You turned as soon as I called your name
my heart wobbling like my knees
when I recognized the back of your head
across the crowded room

You opened your arms
innocent and pleased
I went straight into them, urgent,
my sudden wings
shaking themselves alive
out of my shoulders

Our voices spoke of ordinary things
in the feel of your unshaven cheek against mine
I felt a man's feathered softness
I wanted to rub myself there
as if you were my father
and could protect me

I felt something ripple
through our bellies where we pressed
 my white shirt against your black sweater

As we pulled apart
I wondered if I was blushing

When I felt your breath coming
and going
my heart unfolded
and became a brave white lily

Underneath the Veil

It feels as though I am holding my breath indefinitely
even though that is impossible.

I stand within a mystery
darkness covers my eyelids like a veil

the color of blue twilight
the color of the sky when the first star appears.

The darkness is comfortable:
not to rip the veil away to scorch my eyes

with the sharp tearing sun. And yet there
is nothing I want more than to feel

the sun on my naked skin and
stand in front of you revealed,

nothing hidden, nothing held back.
I am neither afraid nor unafraid.

Simply fall to my knees, the love bursting
out through the cracks in my heart, forcing me

to confession. How the veil falls
onto the opened palms of your hands.

How About Silence?

What if we had no words?
What if the only way we could speak was with the
Expression in our eyes, arch of the eyebrow
Fingers touching
What if you came to me moving in silence
And laid beside me
With roses
What if I held your face in my hands
Like a crystal ball
Seeing the child in you, foreseeing the old man
Appreciating the fine lines
Forming around your eyes
While noting the twinkle
What if I gave myself into your hands
And there were no words to
Distract us
What if each touch was slow and distinct
If each breath formed a hum
A melody, a rhythm
And in the spaces between, only silence

What if we woke up creating patterns
Diagrams, scattered beams of light with our
Hands our legs our backs
Our breath
What if we used taste to tell each other
How much we love, how much we desire
How much we can not, how much we will
What if we swallowed truth like a holy wafer
Made from what we can know
With our blood our salt
Our bones

Continued

What if we no longer were capable of argument
Or misunderstandings
And we could only hear the way our bodies move
Toward each other and away
Like waves on a beach
Like buds opening to day
And folding at night
Like the spin of galaxies
And the journey of the moon
What if we ran out of words
What if we were unafraid to be completely silent?

Our Green Card Anniversary

You come home dressed in black.
I can't decide between silk or
velvet. I remember I wore a lace
blouse. It was a warm October day.
In the photographs I am standing
in shadow, you in the light.

You ask, "Where do you want to go?"
I don't have any appetite, only a desire
to wear stockings and heels and
retrieve the gaze, the way you looked
at me the first time.

I remember how I clutched the flowers,
couldn't call it a bouquet without wanting
to toss it away. In my room there
are tulips and a note. "I want to make
up," you write. The storm was still

ringing in my ears. I remember how we
laughed trying on Halloween costumes
at the party store. One costume was
husband, another wife. I ended up wearing
strands of red coral and a gold

mask. It was our first public
appearance as a married couple.
I hadn't changed my name yet.
The tulips are blooded and I don't know
if I want to rebel or give in because now

I see though your subterfuge. You stood in
the light where the love reflected
off your face for all the memories
to come. I stood in shadow
promising that the tears I accumulate

Continued

would belong to us both. We took it on
despite the clock of abandonment
ticking its warning note.
"I want to make up," you wrote.

"The way I love you is beyond words,"
I write back. At the table you open the card
and I can't read the expression on your face.

On *Dia de los Muertos* your ancestors danced
on the altar with mine. Does that make us family?
Your mother's spirit came by and blessed me in the
shadowy aftermath of the party when we
drank too much tequila. She said you would

never let me go. You hold on by offering
tulips, dinner out, the red wine I like best.
You never said you believed the
vows we took. You took my tears
and braided them into the rug at the entrance

of our home, where I live with
your name that is now mine and my
disappointments. *Dia de los Muertos* is
coming and I am afraid the grief will sweep me
away. Once again you

reach out to catch me. I remember
we drank champagne and I went home alone
and happy. Tonight we drink champagne
and you take me into your life
as neatly as folding shut an envelope.

When I tell you I need you, you
do not try to negate me. I say
I think it is natural. You say, "Are you
ready for tiramisu?"

Do You Still Love Me?

This is my poem to the way we stand:
you looking to horizons, events, future
pastures of plenty, me to you, breathless
and dazed.

This is my poem to the way we
hold our arms around
each other: you lightly
companionable, hospitable

as if it is by accident that it is me,
it could just as well be any,
me wanting nothing more
than to squeeze inside your skin

dissolve like smoke
in morning fog, mutated
into pure fragrance, the taste
of you on my tongue like *rompope*

or *gelato* or anything indescribable
and tender, bruised like fruit
pinched a little too hard, like
lilies crushed against the stone wall,

returned back to myself each and
every time. This is my poem about how
we communicate: you speaking
in a foreign tongue of adventures

off to war in your costume
of flamboyant gestures, me
speaking of the silken pull of spirit
across my heart, finding comfort in

Continued

the way love has upended me
one more time but still able to get back up, smile.
Still able to pick you
out of the crowd, beckoning, mine.

Not Only Fire

How did I emerge from your rib
the very one I slept against next
to your heartbeat, curled and certain.

How did you unfold me
like a paper flower on its long stem
petal by petal, bent back

into deepening color with each
press, until at last the surprised
mouth that did not know until this

moment how much it longed to
drink from yours, the fiery tongue
that tweaks my nerves into flame

those long rolled r's filling
my senses with liquid joy.
How did you emerge out from my

small gesture of sympathy, the tears
I cupped to my heart like a string of
pearls, mine alone, out from the loss

of the oyster. How he moistened the grit
day by day in his underwater depths,
how I learned the way

to pry him open.

Afternoon Poetry Reading

She reads poems. He listens.
She speaks of a poet's life, he nods.
I notice the nod, the look that passes
between them like an unbroken thread.
I notice the thread, the unbroken
look, the red juice of heart blood spattered
on his hands from her words, the star
that appears on her forehead from his look.
I think, how sweet. I am envious.

I know they are married. I imagine
them at the altar, a poem split into two
voices like the shank bone
broken to conform the eternal
covenant of freedom.
"You will be my people. I will be
your God," He told Abraham, bondaging
souls for the trek across the desert
to come. "I will be your woman,
I take you as my man," I imagine her
repeating in front of a long line of ancestors
holding their breath to see it accomplished.
She is not young any more, like me
and I do not know how many nights
she paced, like me, and how many
lovers she kissed and discarded before
this one. A man who loves to
hear her mouth forming words
in the intricate measure of hidden
meaning and sudden story.

I do not know if he had wives
before this one, writes the alimony
check with one hand gripped to the
regret or love spilling out of his insides

like an enchilada casserole with too
much cheese. I do not know how they
found each other whether it was
spontaneous combustion
or a soft remembrance like a dream
on the tip of the mind's edge

But I count the nods, the looks, the pride
I sense coming though the pores of his
skin. I can only see the back of
his head but I already know—
just as someone who is famished
knows what the diner ate by the tilt of
satisfaction in his chin, just as the enslaved
knows what stars would fall
into her hands if she but
slipped off the chains.

Things We Lost In the Fire

The Telephone Call

I did it wrong, I said too much,
I didn't say enough, I should have
waited, I should have listened first,
I should have remembered:
my aspiration is to be a saint.

I waited too long, I should have called
sooner, I should not have called
at all, I drank too much, I asked too
many questions, I took his advice, I heard
my heart's refusal and denial, I woke up
afraid, I forgot to pray, I forgot:
I am supposed to be an angel.

It was the wrong thing to say, I should have
shut up, I should have hung up, I should
have cried foul, I should have said I don't feel
good and I am edgy and out of sorts so let's talk
later, I should have thought ahead, I should
know the difference, I didn't know the anger
flaring up between us would consume the
phone line into ash, I should have kept the
rest of you in mind first because:
my purpose is to Shine The Light.

I did it all wrong, the emails made it
worse, I should have said sorry right
away, I didn't think ahead, I blurted out the
truth, I am not to hurt anyone but
myself, if I knew what was good for me,
anyway, what's to lose if there is nothing
but lies, what is there to hang onto if I am
making a mistake, I woke up instead of realizing:
I was supposed to stay up on your pedestal.

Departure

She rises at dawn
unlocking the doors of
his heart's breath when
she leans over to kiss him good-bye
because he doesn't yet know

if the same as love,
the way he wants her.
She hasn't spoken for days
about it, only the practical,
the grocery list taped

to the door instead of crumpled
into his hand, the mail
piled by the plate instead of
tossed on the couch, the
question about the oil change,

that's how he knows she
is still angry. She has not
again mentioned her desire
to leave him or how her
heart has grown

solid like a rock or like
glass, he can't remember
exactly what she said
only the words were sharp
and hurt. But then

it started from his own
carelessness, he knew
it did. Why did he want
to take it out on her
when she was his

world, why did he say
things just to see his own
frustration mirrored back
but with tears and with
fists plunged into the soft lap

he loved to lie back in,
his head cushioned,
crowned by love, by love
by her soft fragility, the
center where he knew her

strength and her fear.
He knew how to reach her
there, fall into the ocean
of love, of love the place
of consummation by

Life itself, the beat of the
tide's blood, the merging
of two into one
whole. He felt it once
or twice, as vivid as birth

the crowning through the
core into light.
And now she
shielded herself away
from him, she beat her

fists into swords to shape
the words, slicing him
this way and that, how tired she
was of his anger, how she
needed to get away from him. And

Continued

would. The shock as his
breath left him. Knowing these
words were true, knowing
he had lost her,
only a matter of

a ticket to be purchased
on the internet, a suitcase
to be filled. And then
slowly, later, the wonder
that they had been at all

that she had come to him
one day out of cold rain
with her hair dripping and
her mascara streaked and how
he had wanted her and

the joy when she answered
out of her own hunger and the
way she gave herself
without once questioning
that there could be love

born between them as well,
that he could rise up like a
star and grasp all the
wind to encompass her.
And now the door has

clicked shut and he
is afraid to open his eyes
on the scene, the way their life
has suddenly emptied
into one blue backpack

and one green suitcase but
he rolls over and smites
himself on the forehead
and knows that somehow
he must get through the

day and so he awakens.
Somewhere in the room
a rose is shining, somewhere
she has left a piece of
herself.

What He Found In the Garbage

a spatula melted into the shape of Saturday morning pancakes
the cast iron skillet shimmered with rust
one barbeque splashed apron, checkered, gifted, crumbled, torn
one feather duster mugged with dirt
brown boots with split soles, one crumbled sock textured to the grain
twenty CDs scratched and deformed, grinning with melodies
memorized and worn
a date book with a broken spine, pages slashed with black, others
rimmed with red
two cracked wine glasses, one beer stein as silvery as drunken
apologies
a shirt pocket ripped from the pen that signed the divorce papers
a black shoe polish can, rimmed and empty
at the bottom a silver chain, when he pulled it out, a locket
shaped to the size and condition of his heart, tarnished with sin
false bravado, fake accord, lies and sleepless nights, recriminations
born from guilt, secret tears, messages scattered on smoke
one flattened brown cardboard box left under the stairs, a chaos
of cleaning products under the sink, a hornet's nest by the kitchen
window, a lock without a key, a crushed dream, a dance of fire in his
loins, a kiss left upon his pillow, an urge to bellow,
a walk to the sea and throwing his ring into the deep, a walk to
the edge and falling into the wishing well of regret, a drink of
forgetfulness, a hang-over of remembering, and then
lifting his face to the rain

and starting all over again

Exhaustion

I will be a ruby
    embedded in the bowl of your navel
I am an opal
    clinging to the soft lobe of your ear
I am stardust
    flung in your hair
        and rose petals falling on the
            clean white sheets.
I am sunlight
    glazing your limbs with fire
        and the murmur of the sea
            rocking you to distant islands.

So she thought
    humming to herself through the
        loneliness.

The candle flame and hot liquid
    of mulled wine sliding down her
        parched throat
were designed to seduce herself
    into sleep. But what use is sleep
        without dreams?

And in whose eyes does she see herself
    while she tosses and turns
        in the dark?

I will be a ruby,
    she chanted to the silence
        the electric digits of the clock
            the hum of the refrigerator
            in the next room.

Continued

I will be an opal,
      as all the tears collected
            in the bowl of her womb
                  began to dilute her blood.

Waiting After Midnight

I wanted white roses. I wanted rain to
come in the window. The sky was gray
and the moon had disappeared,
the cherries were sweet and chilled.

The roses wept, the rain dripped
down the pane and the
phone never rang,
the bowl filled with cherry pits

and my fingers were crimson.
The moon blew away the clouds
and silvered my solitude,

my pearly body opaque and bold.
I remember the tears
you spilled into the cup of my breasts
to drink when I am thirsty,

the scent of damp earth,
the way the white curtains
rose and fell.

Little Valentines — Love Poems for Valentines Day and Beyond

Promise

My heart waits poised to drink you in
like nectar to a bee
to be a rock pummeled under a waterfall
to be jubilant and outrageous as a
shooting star.

Love cannot be measured,
how brief our stay
in rapture's holy work!

Harmony

Love is a song in the
mouth of my heart as
I awaken first in the
brightness of morning.
I hold fast to this truth as
your body enfolds me
though you hesitate and
I understand
but don't understand

ready to plunge into the flame
prepared for me while I slept.

Joy

I have spent all my wintering
like a black sun burst into flame
the hard edges melted into flowers
   (I want to wear flowers in my hair:
     see how I blaze on the wings
      on this great good morning)
My heart cannot close
        cannot close
         cannot stop this terrible pounding
             this beautiful pounding

Wings

I am restless finding your name
on the tip of my tongue yet unable
to speak it aloud

This feels to be more than flirtation
but I am terrified you will turn away from me
when you uncover the depth of my feeling

When it is the depth of my feeling
that draws me to you like a moth to a flame
My wings are already scorched
My resurrections already begun

A Gift

When I hold out my heart
to you in my small simple
hands, will you...? And will
you know it has been
forged in the fire, purged
by the rain...?

Rapture

A moment before we are
afire, impatient
A moment after we are
breathless, shuddering
Tomorrow
my heart will echo your name

Closer

Because the night is sweet
and you are close, I lean into
the caress of your voice, I lean
my heart right against
yours

Perfect symmetry
of one plus one
is no more than
the beat of my heart
in you, the pulse
of your rhythm
in me.

Menage a Trois

The heart is limitless—
only the molten heat
of the mouth falls
silent as dreams
weave us into
one long
sigh

Solitude

In my own world
a desire to aspire
heart-fire, a love
that draws me close

Not meant to be alone
but no one has soothed
the ache of these arms
yearning to the burning

like a candle flame
in the dark
like a touch of hope
in a wintered heart

Graced

Have I found love:
o tender precious night
and grateful dawn?

I celebrate in you
a cause to live, a grace
bestowed when I thought
my heart had turned
to stone

But now it is engraved
with your name
and sealed til the grave.

Heart Afire

A flame is ignited
by your touch. Pleasure
awakens my heart and
this song becomes a rhythm
of rising and falling. While kisses
surge between our breaths,
we are consumed but
not burnt, this offering
made to man by God.

Reflection

Mirrors are false: they reflect me
separate and alone
when I know I am woven
into this one heart we have birthed,
that we devour with kisses
and sighs.

Sorrow

What do you want me for?
You only play
My heartstrings resonate
Under your restless fingers
Drawing forth a melody
I can only be mocked by

Pierced

I am not satisfied
with promises, I want
your kisses to transgress
the boundaries again
and again, little arrows
straight to the heart

Surrender

I yearn to hold you as close as the
blood in my veins, to mark
the boundaries with kisses
and to rock you with the
rhythm of the moon within me.
You my heart, you my
soul's delight.

Sitting By the Hearth

Like a Blaze of Fire

(a past life memory)

I stand in the dark, place of hidden regrets
alone, waiting, remembering.
For how many centuries stood thus a woman
veiled, censored, the nun's rustle, a cross tied to a belt.
Quietly cool in contemplative prayer.
And beneath, a passion for God
that splays her hard on rough stone
until her bones crack from the heat
of her blazing soul.

In *el pasillo*
she passes by the other woman
her friend, the exiled one, *la conversa*,
from a Jewess to a Catholic
by baptism of tears,
dark in her lace and velvet gown
in this place where dreams meet to yearn
for a kind look, a word, a nod, a touch.

La Señorita waits for the priest to pass by. She lowers
her head, modest, hands clasped
demurely. He does not know the tight marks
drawn by a knife on the delicate skin
of her thigh. One for every denied kiss,
every thrust of the blade in her heart when
he does not glance her way.

The sun beats down. Soon it will cross
the flagstones, lay a message of liquid gold
more precious than the rubies she wears
on her fingers, the pearls in her hair.
She will stand in it, her arms spread open
to catch the wind.

Continued

She imagines daughters running
in the garden, the innocent love she will
bind to herself as tightly as vows.
A secret smile as she passes
the nun in the shaded corridor, her friend
exiled for the love of God. They nod,
a word, a touch. The fragrance of
gardenias fills the molten air.

Dear Cordoba, I Want You

not only the way a woman yearns
to trace the contours of her man's face
not only the way she yearns to feel
the hot throb of his heartbeat
under her hand
but with total abandoned pleasure.
I want to saunter over your mysterious
cobbled streets having thrown my watch away
aimless, lost deliberately, without haste.
I take with me the burning *palmas* and sharp cries
crescendoing across the plaza that accompany
the thin dark guitarist
who never once looked in my direction
and yet as surely as I know my bones
elongate in the late afternoon sun
he is singing to me the plaintive ancient
songs and he knows this has unfolded my soul
from its hiding place to dance without shame
to his fire. These cries I wear next to my skin
as I search for a cool garden to rest in.
I want pink roses to wear in my
hair and to carry in my worn
hands like a pledge to the
altar of your golden age
while I am awakening to the
golden tilt of your sun.
I want you, Cordoba, the way a woman
wants her lover to enter her, softly with
the intention to stay, to fill her with joy
and to keep her close, no matter the
distance or the passage of time.

Jerusalem

She is the place of all my dreams
why can I not be there?
I entered her in sackcloth and ashes,
I departed in mourning, weeping,
kissing, taking with me the heart
of one of her true sons.
Good enough for him,
why can't I be good enough for her?
Is my heart too pure for
her blood-stained streets or too fragile
for the blood lust that she evokes?
Devoted to her vision,
I was humiliated, threatened and scorned
and yet no one succeeded in hurting me.
I laughed with joy
at the miracle of her very being,
her revenge on her destroyers,
from ashes she arose
a celestial carrousel
now poems, now daggers,
now screams, now prayers.
I dream of her but she denies me.
I reach out for her but she turns me away.
In the thin light of morning
I beseech her name and her pity.
When will I sit beside
her moon-washed gates
and be enchanted by her
midnight splendor?
When will I be able to touch her heart
and be touched by the secret
she guards so severely?
Must I wait until she is worthy
of a man of peace,
must I wait until I am

strong enough
to stand against her,
to become equal to her danger
and demand that she be holy?

For My Son, on His 23rd Birthday

There is an ache in my arms
when no child is near. When I was
young, the ache was about wings

and flying but you taught me
the beauty of mothering, of
flesh warm and innocent

smelling of promise and
the little boy trust of which
I am unworthy and must become.

I wanted girls, imagining dolls
and dress-ups. Instead the closet
was filled with cars and trucks,

their hard metallic bodies screeching
and zooming. I did not know
what to do when you struggled

into and out of messes. I had no
idea that childhood could be
so hard. But I did know not

to panic the day you came home
with blood dripping down
your face and shirt, the hour in the

hospital awaiting x-rays the
longest in my life, longer
than the agony of your birth.

When we got home, the elderly
neighbor had washed the stairs of
blood. Gratefully I noticed

because I was exhausted
by fear and incapable of doing one
thing more, although I brought you

supper, afraid to touch the
stitched-up bump, afraid of the chasm
my heart had become.

Across the Miles

My love, small
is the window that
opens to your face,
a photograph propped
up by my bed.
Your voice is only a
recollection, I imagine
it as the voice of my son,
seed from his loin that you are.
That is the only way
I can know you,
through what childhood he had
passing along our
blood and memories. But still
Love fills the miles
between us because we
are learning that love
has no rules, no
borders, no gatekeepers,
no perspective, no reason
and no end. We are
learning that no matter
I can only pretend
to know the being you
are through the way
I adore the photo, the
bits of news I get, the
sound of laughter or crying
in the background
of the phone call, still

love is a plant—
love grows without
caring what color the
flower that
will
finally
bloom.

Cater-cousin

When you find me at the bottom—
When you find the grief sealed shut
as a grave, without shadow
or shine, a place only gods

touch and yet leave no trace—
When night steals the kiss
from my lips and the perfume from
my breasts and thighs

and the old aching hunger is put to rest—
When I am empty and silent
as a bell tied to the monk's
matins clamor while midnight

curves its hands around my neck—
when I am filled with surrender
as infinite as mercy—
when I am unfurled like a river

cresting the green banks
of a garlanded summer, will you
come to me, creature and king,
secret and soul, will you whisper

to me all the things I must know,
all that I have been
waiting to hear, will you take me
home and never let go?

Consecration

Consecration

You O God! would You lead me only to betray me?
You O God! would You require all my love and never
    could I feel the healing touch of passion's flame
    for to heal this heart of mine
     to heal this heart's wild rue
     O this life! O this my life!
     I am calling out to You!
For without hope to love, what am I?
     I am not a favored saint who can fast from it
     without breaking
I am already breaking
     can you feel the knife edge at my throat
     can you feel the knife edge of despair
        like the shiver of a grave

widowed with never a consummation
to fill the long emptiness where a man's arms
would be warm around my enchanted womanhood

where mouths speak of truths beyond words
where a spring seed rises up my woman's limbs
and womb and warm wetness in exultation

Holy this moment! Holy O God this consecration!
     where wedded is welded is fused is life-filled
     is joy where weeping can bring no further comfort
     where I take thee this man to be the mirror of my soul

what good does it do to cry to God
unless He formed us
    from the dust from the rib from the breath
    to complete his Holy task
    to bring forth love in all it glory
    to give a hand to a world
    tainted by hate torn by war trashed by greed

Continued

to comfort a wounded world with a gesture
with a word with a life with a being
that we are that we become that we discover
in a moment not secret or contrived
of your eyes meeting mine to find
a sublime truth that was unknown to us before

Wrestling with the Angel

When you broke me open, I didn't yet know
what dawn would filter through the cracks.
I didn't yet know the pain of birth

would rip me apart, that the birthing of myself
began not with a kiss or a conversation
not even with love—

It was too bright to call it by name, it was majestic
although at times I call it gold, sometimes my star and
sometimes hot white light. These words are inadequate

as if I am using sign language in a roomful of blind people.
When you broke me open it was an awakening; today I
say you are the beam of the lighthouse guiding me to the shore

of my own being. I seem to insist on words—they pass along
in emails sailing delirious in cyberspace and letters that sit
for days on my altar before I find courage to send them

and once in a while I am able to use my voice
to say these words and then some other dimension
opens up in me. But the words imprison, the images

useless to this great work. I know you have been used by God
to bring me a message and I know I have fallen in love with the
messenger, hoping it will bring me closer to

remembering a song that is really all mine.

Synopsis

I wanted to tell you this. So long I had been
waiting, not telling. No way to reach the end
of the bridge without tripping over my own.
It is always the truth that catches us. Life
net and web. Frozen dew reflects
sunlight. How often have I pressed this
to my heart, to my lips in prayer,
forming between us
sanctuary.

But it is no use to go back over the past.
If we do not travel forward into what
we can become, we have no business
remembering. The golden thread
hidden in a remnant of carpet. Pull it
and does the weaving unravel or
burst into light? Be innocent
of motive. The force of your
love. The gift of simply feeling.
Not before or after.
Only this.
True.

Serpents and Doves

When I am with you, I am innocent
and wise, back to the girl I was
before the dark time of pain
before the hearth fire was banked
with the peat of despair

innocent like a heart opened wide so that the secrets
tumble out as if they are cascading
ribbons of silk fallen from the sewing box
or a slinky navigating the steep steps
by its own twisty shape

or innocent like a child who lifts her face
to the rain, opens her mouth
and exclaims, A drop went inside!
I am wise like a shooting star sacrificing

its glitter for the compost-hugged root
or a cool hand on the forehead when
the fever drains the body of reason, an inner
knowing of when to be silent and still

When I am with you, the girl needs no hiding place
between purity and defilement
She wears herself proudly
She invites all who pass by to dip
into her storehouse

of bread and wine because she no longer
needs to hoard
for the coming of
bared bones

The Ring

It was only a ring, silvered
   in the shine of rain, invisible
      against the umbrella handle,
         a simple circle and stone

           Of malachite warmed by the
              nerve that travels from my
                heart to my fingertip
                  and back again.

It came off my finger, undone
   in the seeding time when I took
      the tears and planted them
         in the soil of regret

           Only to find brambles grew and
              on every branch a promise frayed
                as the Tibetan prayer flags on
                  the porch of my friend's house

Where we laughed in defiance of
   disappointment. She told me
      she had none left, she had
         set them free as surely

           As she was about to do to her earthly
              body, merging into her true
                worth. Only a bit of silver,
                  token of what I claimed and gave

When I placed my soul in
   his hands. We touched eternity
      like lightning flashing a purple
         warning of storms to come,

As if safe harbor could be the ending
to this story. I wanted garnets
and pearls but there were
none to be had so I dreamed

them, conjured them
in our voices telling each other
what I wanted to believe:
you belong to me
till death do us part.

Death of a friend, death of
a dream, death close to the edge and
only the sweet taste of a
strawberry in my mouth*

Or would I throw this ring
into the dark sea and reach
out instead to the other,
the elusive one made of gold

Beyond my heart, beyond this lifetime

* this refers to a Buddhist teaching: A man is chased over a cliff by
a hungry tiger. He is snagged on a tree branch which then begins to
slowly break. But then, ah! he finds a wild strawberry and places it in
his mouth.

Dancing With the Dark

(for two voices)

I am night
                    I am the day.
I am the unknown.
                    I am precise.
I am a mystery, a shadow, your own dark face.
                    I am obvious. Powerfully I plant my
                    feet in front of the line. I do not step
                    across it and I do not obey.
I weave a perfume of ardor and kisses.
                    I succumb. Only to the degree I am able
                    to carry you away.
I melt in your trembling.
                    I come back to my senses, betrayed,
                    unknown to myself, aching.
I soften and pull us back to the center.
                    I am filling you, forsaken, forsworn,
                    forgiven.
I am the bursting honeysuckle, a bramble, a lily,
a rose with its thorns.
                    I am the crazed firefly, quickened in the
                    night sky, sending out a pattern
                    of mating, a thrill of light.
                    I am the stone at the water's edge,
                    beaten by surf and wind to a craggy
                    shape, covered with lichens, star-fish,
                    sun-scorched and brave.

I am a tempest passing through your
canyons to sculpt them into echoes.
A blade that slices both ways, a heart-ache of silk,
a pillow of velvet and tinsel.

> I lay my head down for a crown.
> I lay down my soul for a glimpse of
> your nakedness.

I am the delta and you are the river.

> You are the storm and I am the lighthouse.

We are both wind and Her magic flute.

Riddle

This is a love that has burned me,
consumed me, harvested me like a
wild bracket of grapes
to be trampled into wine. I am the wine,
I am the goblet blown from the crystalline
fire, I am the fire kindled from root,
I am the mouth that speaks in these riddles.
This is the love that cast me to my knees,
breathless and blackened like a tree
limb burnt on the hearth. I am the hearth,
the ash consummation, the warming of
bones, the coming of light. This is the love
that cast me into silver, molten pledge of illusive
grace, destined for beauty, destined for breath,
found in a treasure box of memory. I am the memory,
I am the song that pierces the twilight
and calls to the sky, I am the flute,
I am the river, I am the love that
weaves its way home.

Lies

My heart is a liar
says I will love you no matter
the cost. Says love can't leave
us stranded when it is

the bridge between us, says
romance is unnecessary, we
know the score

My heart is a lyre, wants to sing
all day even when it is splintering
into fine pieces, wants to make
hymns and praise and alleluias

even when no one is listening, wants
to croon a country ballad, wants to
screech a metal rock anthem to lust

My heart looks for love whenever
it is not busy thrumming, throbbing
sighing, my heart wants us all to
remember we are as wise as

blessing, as dumb as desire. My heart
says I will love you even when you
leave me, even when we're wrong

Not Your Angel

I don't want to be your angel
any more. I don't want to be
made of pure beaten gold or
cold marble or warm clay,
who says we are born of light?

And I don't want to keep
my halo or my wings. I want
to remove them, hang them
in the closet, close the door,
breathe at once the

earthy scent of skin pocketed
with sweat, the places
of sadness fallen into the
cracks of my pleasure, the tracery
of scars upon the heart

finally soothed into sleep.
I don't want to be good
or sweet or gentle. I want the
shadow like the salt of
a margarita, the bite of

tequila after the sour *limón*.
I want to be a flirt, a tease
a run for your money, Pandora
opening her box of treasures,
Aphrodite offering a bite

of apple and daring you closer
the fruit of the tree scattered
under the branches
while we lose everything
but the joy.

Transformation

Waiting For the Miracle

I would give you all I have:
I would give you this winter day
that chokes against the spring,

the light falling snow, the grey.
We looked out the window and praised
the blessed sky for giving in at last.

"Con la fe, hasta la agua cura," he said
and we laughed, then changed it:
"With faith, even laughter heals!"

Last night out in the dry-boned yard
and the dry-boned street and the
dry-starred sky, we held up our

hands imagining snow.
We woke to wind tapping
against the glass on white branches,

the miracle we took for granted
not so long ago. I would give
you the sky with its imponderable blue

warming to daffodils and green.
I would make a bouquet
from all the songs my blood can sing:

yearning and desire and fascination
and flight to present to you
tied with a ribbon of moonlight.

I would give you the dust of a New Mexican
street to wipe off on the seat of your
jeans and sunset flames to hunker down

by, a stray coyote crossing the road
oblivious of traffic and what shuffles
under his feet is not pebbles and dirt.

I would give you time to lay your head
against my heart and think of nothing
but rain and the birds calling

to announce their newly hatched young;
I would shelter you and feed you on
honeysuckle and apricots.

I would give all that I have:
the lazy caress of a river meandering
between mossy banks, the squeeze of sand

between my toes, the rush over ancient rocks.
I would let you swim there in the tadpole lanes,
I would find a way to bring you home.

Communion

I drink you
held to the mouth like a cup
smelling of joy and apricots
I spin in the heat of sunflowers
turning to mark the light
I yield to you
and the mandala of your arms
unfolding me in a design
that is ancient and apostolic

The world shakes and trembles in fear
with pain, with blood red teeth sunk
into earth's dark breast
O how she long to comfort them
lay her hands blackened with
loamy earth, ash and fire
but they turn away, turn back
turn to the terror caused by their greed
the hollowness that demands
human sacrifice

But I tremble in a golden dance
that shakes my tambourine into the soles
of my feet and clamors for more wine
despite the intoxication of one glance
from your eyes

The world aches and wails
and we lick the tears from her wound
we have drowned in the sacred wells
bowered with sharp-thorned berry bushes
We have emerged as fisherman
ready to cast our nets
to catch the stars

The Tarot Reading

Did she say star or did she say cross?
And this detail the least of what she said.
The fat slick deck clicked in my hands
while I concentrated on my question.
Or am I concentrating on the answer
I want? I want her to say,
"Oh, yes, he loves you
and everything will be lovely and fine."
How foolish can this heart possibly
get? That one, the clown card,
bursts in my eyes like sun from
behind the clouds,
the ones I think will never
go away. Isn't that the Fool?
She is speaking words of wisdom,
explanation, logic. I am not listening:
I am dancing like a wild woman
set loose into the garden,
the door, the secret locked door,
broken open
at last.

Mud Wrestling

inspired by Rumi

O my friends, I am mad with love and no one sees
how sweetly I am harnessed to the yoke; this
burden is light as hummingbirds nudging the
Goddess into flight, and O my friends, that
woman is me!

O my friends, I would not speak these words
flavored by flower-petal soup carried
to my doorstep in a Chinese basket
if they were not as true and naked as
the woman leaning back into snow,
if they had not been burnt alive on
my parchment tongue.

You are my friend, he says, and why do
these words make me mad—
I have held out my heart like an ancient
dancer somersaulting against a windowpane,
first yes, then no
first enough, then desire
first I appear next to him in a photograph:
someone says husband-wife and hits the flash:
then I disappear like snow furrowing into mud.

That word scarved back over his shoulder, Friend,
makes me delirious because the echo
in my sea-shell heart says: Awaken, my beloved, and
be like a stag upon the mountains.

I am a woman unraveling myself in a snake dance:
the spiral in my belly wants to snag him
into loving me but each gyration returns me
to my own center. Adoration makes me free

to say friend when I mean I am tuning my life to
the strumming of his fingers, to say solitude
when I mean I am hoping to learn harmony.

The Sound Of My Name

In the middle of the night
I awaken
to hear my name
spoken softly
and so sweetly
I fall out of insomnia
into a dream
fall back onto the pillow
so sweetly
the longing
and the loneliness
fall off of me
cushioned softly
like a hand-picked star.

In the hot tub
I close my eyes
yearning to hear
that voice calling me
my limbs floating
in womb warmth
my head silvered
by the moon
and my dark wedge of hair
reminding the night
I have not yet
turned back into mermaid.
I am still human
and woman
and nearing to a time
of utter solitude
when no one
but the wind can give
me answers.

I float and a kiss
falls so softly
on my lips
I am awakened
out of insomnia
I am held
like a hand-picked star
in the great arms
of what it is impossible
to name
even though
it is apparent
that he knows mine
by heart.

Call Me Beloved

And did you get what you wanted
from this life? Even so, I did.
What did you want? To call myself
Beloved, to be beloved on this earth."
Raymond Carver

All I wanted was to be called Beloved
You can say friend and it chimes true
as the wind chimes on the balcony
in a night of tears reminding me
out beyond my self there is the wind,
there is an arroyo, stars and a
highway to a land I have yet to see

All I wanted was to hear the word Beloved
softy whispered like a child
saying, "I want my mommy," the sleep
still flushed on her cheeks and mine
the only lap in sight

I wanted to chew that word like
a croissant in a French café
warm and flaky in a blue dish
and no one across the table but you,
leaning towards each other in the midst
of a language we do not understand
but are illuminated by like light through a window
made of stained glass

I wanted that word to follow me down
the aisle of the movie theater
your hand on my back and the popcorn
spilled and crunchy at the first sign
of laughter, our shoulders meeting in
common accord that it is we who
bought the tickets and chose
this place beside one another

All I wanted was to be called Beloved
out of gratitude, like a prayer, to hear the
name I was born with, not the one given
to me by a distraught teen-aged mother, but to hear
the sound of my real name in your mouth,
my real calling, my destiny, to stand
in the place where I am both mirror and veil

Sunday Afternoon

Hold me, rock,
hold me the way I need to be held:
firm, determined, loyal.
Take my heart-ache
and mold it into sand,
break it into earth.
Take the running waters of my grief
and soak the forest with its nectar.
Take my bones, kiss them back
into effervescence, into freedom.
Help me remember I am only
Light borrowing this flesh
for one brief moment, one
brief life.
Hold my sorrow in the cup
of your courage.

Hold me, rock, in the
sacred shape of compassion.
How the Divine saw that it was good....
To be a man, to be a woman, and thus
to yearn for the whole.

Only Light

You do the things they say
will help. Say the prayers, light
the candles, wear a Santo on a

string around your neck, blest by a priest.
Cast stones enscripted with your fears
into the river. Stand still watching

sunsets, count the
steps to the center of the
labyrinth with each measured

breath. You can't stop
the slow fusion of destiny with
you own skin and bones. There

is no way to foresee the joy
you might inherit as simply
as lying back on a blanket

to look up at the vast sky and there
is no way to foretell
the sorrow that will clamp

you shut. The walk to the center,
the days on the edge. The long gaze
into the fire— how can you know.

Still you can't stop the attempt
each time to find who you really
are and who you are becoming.

You light this candle in hope
and knowing, this is the way
home, this is the way.

Turning 50

With luck a salter's fire,
with luck a loving hand, wine
in the cup, companionship.
With luck, next to the lime tree
grasping the key to a vision and

no time to hold back.
Nothing to gamble with but hope,
nothing to earn but fate and fortune,
the sharp penny of hindsight
more valuable than the pearls cast away.

The heart of the matter:
kissing life full on the mouth:
stones and trees, gentle-breasted birds,
seascapes, mountain streams, ice-lake,
sunsets that splash and shimmer and fade

the way an infant is cradled,
the way the child asks about stars,
the way hurt shatters, the way betrayal
burns, the way we cry on our knees,
the things of this world that shape us

and the blade of rescue and the
wings of escape, flung free to the wind,
flung free to come home again.

About the Author

In 2004, Wendy Brown-Báez released her poetry CD *Longing for Home* and since then, has performed poetry nationally and in Mexico, in unique venues such as cafes, galleries, schools, and cultural centers, solo and in collaborations. She has published poetry in dozens of literary journals including *Borderlands, Out of Line, The Litchfield Review, The Awakenings Review, Blue Collar Review, Sin Fronteras, Wising Up Press, Minnetonka Review, Mizna,* and on-line journals *Lunarosity,* and *Flask and Pen.* Wendy is the creator of **Writing Circles for Healing** writing workshops. She received a 2008 McKnight grant to teach a bilingual writing/performance workshop.

She is available to speak to your book club, writer's group or workshop. To get in touch with her: www.wendybrownbaez.com

Wendy believes our true home is in the arms of the Divine and in the center of our being, but her earthly homes are in Minneapolis, Santa Fe, and Puerto Vallarta with family and friends.

Printed in the United States
136359LV00002B/9/P

9 780911 051087